COLORLESS SOCIETY
(A COLLAGE OF THOUGHT)

J. P. Bartley

To order additional copies of this book, contact:
Xlibris
844-714-8691
www.Xlibris.com
Orders@Xlibris.com

ISBN: Softcover   978-1-4415-3680-8
           Hardcover   978-1-4415-3681-5
           EBook   979-8-3694-3883-1

Library of Congress Control Number: 2009904697

Print information available on the last page

Rev. date: 01/15/2025

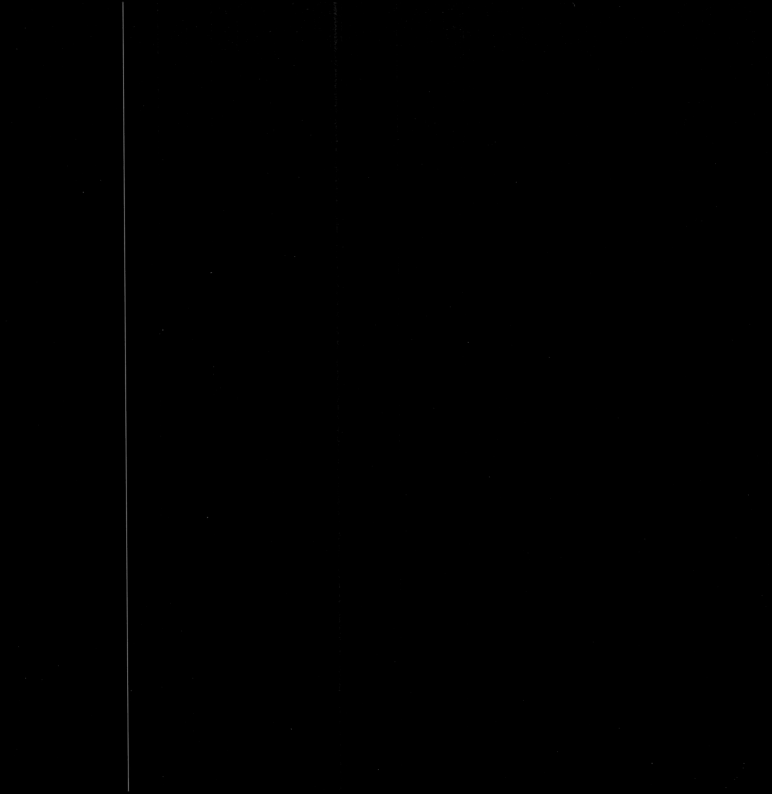

Imagine life without color

4

No
red
stains or odors
of red roses...

Just

plain

roses

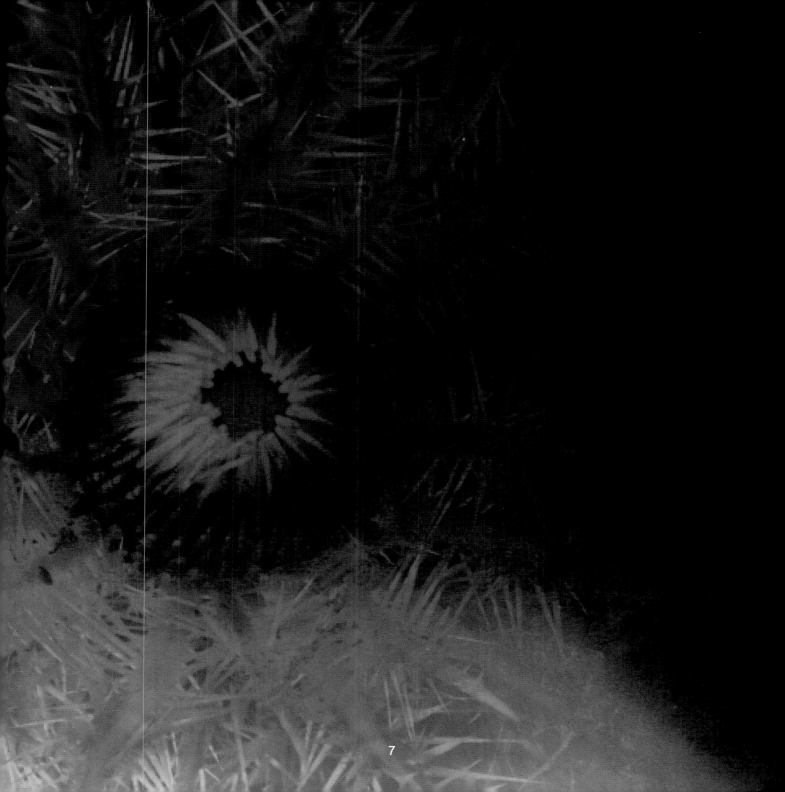

Absent
of
all shades

Waters
Oils

Even
Pastel

As
an autumn
too dry with no
pigment to
display,

And such bitter

chaos to be human once more ,
How I long for racial dispute;
True dilemma that lies True, yet
obviously negative and musters
reproach,
Where there is hurt there is
truth and an absence of
iridescence,

How
many will
learn to hurt in
happiness,
As I have smiled and put
away my mental discomfort till
the morrow,
For tomorrow knows nothing of
today's happiness,
As happiness of today knows nothing of
tomorrow,

Each looking toward the denial of each,
With ignorance to time and direction,
Sleeping at the leisure of sleep itself.

Wake up!

Wipe the fog from your
eyes,

Look
beyond the
scales,
   -See it-
If I took your arms and legs
would you not still be able?
Yet, you can not,
I'd have to snatch your sight before
you could truly see it,

For it is all an illusion, a manipulation
of my personal fantasy!

Colorless

Society

The Long Road
Home

As I travel the long road home again, a road to which I know
no end,
Coming up along the way I saw a river bend,
I ran to get a closer look and got a cup to drink,
A drink so good it made me cry, Lord, I know I'm not worthy,
This is true He said to me, but still I love you so,
Gather your things, leave the cup, it is again your time to go.

Road

To

Reality
Vol. 1

The following is a dream. I include this because I am first and far most a dreamer. Secondly, I'm less afraid, these days, of sharing my dreams.

...I was seemingly on a fence or a piece of a wooden deck. Whatever it was we were moving very briskly. I say we because it seemingly had a very large portion of extended family and others that I lived with at the time. It kind of felt like every one I knew, because in addition to those I lived with friends would peek around the shoulders of family. I think every one on board thought that I was in control. I was seated in the front center and felt as if I should be driving but there were no controls. However I felt did not matter because I was most certainly, not in control. We were catapulted out of a whirlwind and seemed to be attached to a rope as we moved about. We were very close to the ground and at some times throughout the dream I thought that the wooden "thing" we were on had to have wheels. At other times, because there was an up and down motion consistently, it felt as if we were skipping like a rock would on water. We came to another tornado looking whirlwind. I did see it but could not avoid it. Hence, we ran smack in the middle of it. It turned us about, shook us up a good bit, and catapulted us in the direction we'd come from. The whirlwind had zero visibility inside and when we came out there were less people on board. Though there's less people at this point, there's still a ridiculous amount of people on board considering that we were on a wooden deck bobbing up and down at an even faster pace than before. I found myself at this point calling out to talk to who was in control. This was very unintentional. I simply verbalized my confusion by saying, 'what is this'. At the time it wasn't a question because I didn't expect a response; from... me or anyone on board. I said this as the craft we were on was yet accelerating and we were about to crash into yet another tornado looking whirl wind. We didn't miss! Who ever was in control was consistent. Just as before the whirl wind shook me up then spit us out; faster and of course with less family on board. I said a second time 'what is this' and heard a voice say "now your headed toward the truth". I can say that what I heard was the answer to my question, but I was still on a wooden deck with a bunch of family members going really fast. [*The rope may be significant; it seemed to be attached to whatever was in control. The controller of our moving craft was well ahead of us and unseen. The rope disappeared before crashing into the last storm.*] Though I heard the voice, I still didn't understand what that meant in relation to the matter at hand. And I figured that "truth" must have been the name of the next tornado looking whirl wind that we were headed for; it was massive and just as cloudy as the previous ones. We smacked it, this time after being shook up the dream dissolved.

I had this dream in the late nineties. I'm still not sure sometimes what it means and I'm not too anxious to slap a meaning on it. This dream has stayed in my memory for a long time. I include it here because it involves storms and truth. Apparently in my search for truth and as I journey home, storms are necessary.

Jesus! got any hope?

got any hope...

a glimpse, a cluster... show me a sign... rain...fire,

crop duster, a helicopter; rescue me... stop the... (stop the) gangsters playing hiphoppers, politicians playing doctor, kids playing murderer, wiches praying blessings, saints spitting curses stolen verses fill their purses sampling schemes and themes my last nerve cauterized they sampled my dreams shameless games and mascarades that people play all my leaders and teachers, prophets and preachers, so called healers pointed me to themselves; turned themselves to hope stealers.

Hey dope dealer,

give me some hope; name your price...

you sure that's the cost?

19

You sure that's the cost?
This is nice but I feel like I'm being tossed; hey
Boss if you didn't carry hope why didn't you say so?
Sticking me with this crack ... Now I'm wide open
only started with a gap,
I'm loosing my teeth, My Heart don't beat,

I'm all alone chief. The void that was a gap is now a
hole in my soul chief... a hole in my soul.

Just a little hope
I'm at the end of my- smoke, Oh God, the rope is
on fire, Put out an "A P B" calling all cars is... there
any hope. ====== Tell Phillip ask Morris; why
I'm, nervous and anxious, acting a fool, I need the
wisdom of Kings but it seems that they need filters,
lost my cool sucking down polluted hope as I choke
I surrender,

Hey Bartender...
Set me up, No-not soda pop, I'll take a triple, a
double, a drop.
Hope

Hennesy on purple eyes he says,

Hope I say
"Hope?!" He says,

Enough Jack to jack you up into outer space,
Not high as the heavens, endless turns like figure
8's,
Hook you with a dead end 7
"Nope" he says
"No hope" he says
And splash goes my face into...1...2...4...8...
Pieces.

Hey sweetness,

I like your smile, maybe we can talk for a couple of
miles,
Maybe there's something that we can do, to bring you
hope and me some too,

I thought you'd understand but you didn't, I feel more
helpless now than I felt in the beginning.

Tell me, have you ever felt this...

helpless... rejection...
Some one help me I'm mellllting.

I feel hopeless from the brokenness...
Pain and suffering...
Always feeling empty...

Always missing something... I'm tired of the void transactions
and sinful actions I need grace, to make it in this
place, save more than my face,
Looking to the stars in outer space
Jesus if your listening, I'll do whatever it takes whether
Baptism or Christening,
Whether Purgatory ain't, isn't, or Is. Wherever you are
Jesus is where I want to live.
I don't care if I have to suffer, condition me to take the
heat like a muffler, I'll grit my teeth before I pucker,
Jesus hear me please... forgive me please

I'm open...

Hope n.

*I wrote the above in august of 2005, a week before my family
and I would evacuate for what became the country's worst
disaster.*

A Medley (New Orleans)

I loved you,
I gave you all you asked for,
You said you wanted some body new,
My daddy told me 'bout women like you
Everyday you say "Come back tomorrow",
Every night balm for my sorrow,
With your sweet scintillating promises,
Standing idly by while I try and try

Cry cry Cry

Is it love,
Cause I can't read between the signs,
Your dance has got me dazed,
I admit, I am helplessly hypnotized
The song you sing, says that things will be
just fine
I wake up feeling alone wiping glaze from
my eyes,
I can faintly see you're singing a different

The dance I hear the strange steps seem so far gone
It has no sweet rhyme
My eyes can't recognize and goes on and on,
and on, must be a secret song,
Reminds me of times I get confused and suspect
some kind of wrong,
in days far gone,
Now I'm, searching the depths of my mind,
Playing back the dates and all of the times,
I can't help thinking that maybe,
Oh how she slays me,
She might be
giving me
Soliloquy

She just might be giving me Soliloquy,
To tell me bye-bye
don't even try
Cry, Cry, Cry

Put on some old records and cry
Your boys can't see
Your girl can't hear
Least you can say you tried
Sing out your soul
Tune out your tears
Be free
Sobs brake the notes
you can call it a riff
Be happy and free don't ask why
Cry, Cry, Cry

I Send...

I sent a message of love there was
no answer,
I persisted and pursued as
though my heart and my hands
were,
made of Steel, my love was
strong that's why I'm here,
but the flames and the heat like
oxygen and acetylene to a spark,
in the space of vulnerability
imploded my heart,
My universe is all over the place,
I knew I took a risk,
Now I'm hurting in galaxies I
didn't even know exist, and the
twist,
I still love
From here to there I still love
over, under, and in-betwixt
I will love got to love I want to
love you.
I send my kindness and loaded
gifts of love,
Loaded with hope and ill formed
expectations,
I think of far off places and when
I'm not I'm thinking of your
face,
How my heart races
I send my patience and one way
love is all I know so I'll include
a self addressed stamped return
receipt; circle yes or don't circle
no,

Interception

*I've sent a message of my own that
did not reach your heart.
Exposing my own vulnerability
longing for your love.
There is a question I must ask
regarding
this message you speak of.
Was it written clearly and in plain
color?
Or tell me my love, was this
message sent to another?*

*Is it my face that makes your heart
race?
Is it me you love over, under and
in-betwixt
Or is my longing for your love just
an ex-lover's wish?*

I Send... Again

I'm sending signals shaken,
stirred, and mixed,
If this doesn't work I'll send a
wish,
Selfish as I am don't wish a wish,
Be my answer,

Be my yes,
Be the missing peace,
The missing joy,
The one,
My rising from the East.

Skeletal Bubbles

Such fragility, the water evaporates and all that if left is
gone,
Weak as a new born fawn,
Falling in and out of air, its end is clear and near,
Fading till it no-longer appears,
Falling as tears they seem to seer where they may crawl,
Scars left fossilized on the bathroom wall.

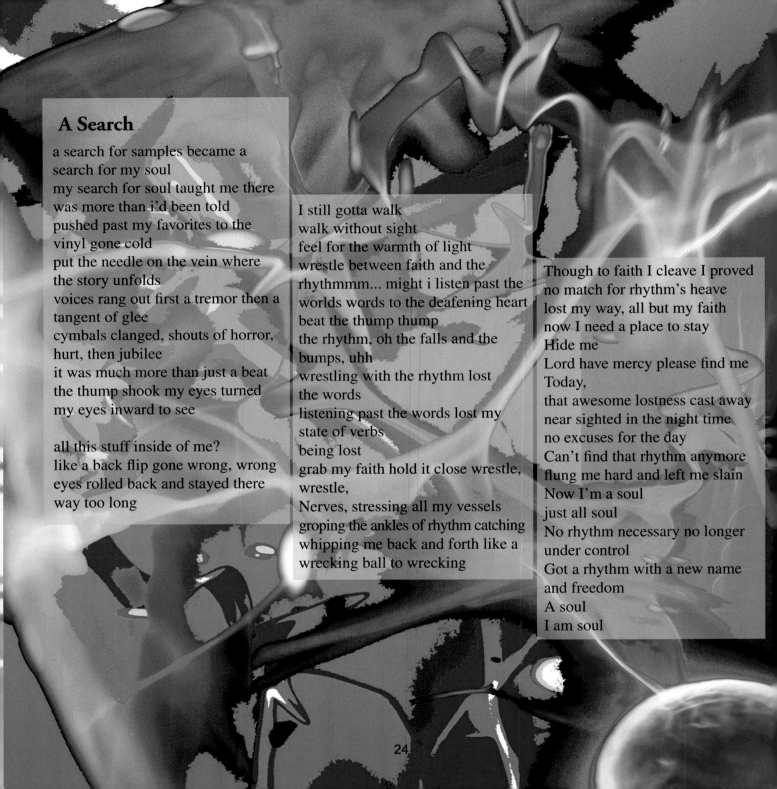

A Search

a search for samples became a
search for my soul
my search for soul taught me there
was more than i'd been told
pushed past my favorites to the
vinyl gone cold
put the needle on the vein where
the story unfolds
voices rang out first a tremor then a
tangent of glee
cymbals clanged, shouts of horror,
hurt, then jubilee
it was much more than just a beat
the thump shook my eyes turned
my eyes inward to see

all this stuff inside of me?
like a back flip gone wrong, wrong
eyes rolled back and stayed there
way too long

I still gotta walk
walk without sight
feel for the warmth of light
wrestle between faith and the
rhythmmm... might i listen past the
worlds words to the deafening heart
beat the thump thump
the rhythm, oh the falls and the
bumps, uhh
wrestling with the rhythm lost
the words
listening past the words lost my
state of verbs
being lost
grab my faith hold it close wrestle,
wrestle,
Nerves, stressing all my vessels
groping the ankles of rhythm catching
whipping me back and forth like a
wrecking ball to wrecking

Though to faith I cleave I proved
no match for rhythm's heave
lost my way, all but my faith
now I need a place to stay
Hide me
Lord have mercy please find me
Today,
that awesome lostness cast away
near sighted in the night time
no excuses for the day
Can't find that rhythm anymore
flung me hard and left me slain
Now I'm a soul
just all soul
No rhythm necessary no longer
under control
Got a rhythm with a new name
and freedom
A soul
I am soul

Day-Time Moon

Can't
find my
way,
Could you
offer any kind
words to say?
Some wise counsel, if
you'd oblige;
Teachings to impart,
A thought to sooth a troubled
mind;
To chase the toils of sufefring hearts,
Pardon, Okay,
Well perhaps I should talk to my God,
Yet you sit FULL in my face;
given charge over night moving in on my days,
Thought I'd glean a little something to quench the sour
taste,
Seeing as you witness my plight through this maze,
And just Why is it that I'm howling at you;
Don't ask me, I thought you'd HAVE a clue.
Or two, or maybe you do,
Non-willing witness no cofession for my confusion?
What, no help with my conelusions; Daytime Moon collusion
Well, guess I will talk to God.
Get some answers round here, you'll see
Find out why you'RE not where you'RE supposed to be
Why can't you just give a little more light
Look up in the daytime and you're illuminating slight CAN'T BE RIGHT
Taunting and pouncing behind every tall building as the sun shines- silly...
me to duck and hide naked and nilly, There's no concealing
A NAKED STATE OF MIND
Night falls into day and my way STILL I cannot find.

Hope of the Broken Tree

Like water to extremely thirsty, but not dry, cacti.
Life may have made me a little prickly, but I did ask
to be tempered to take the heat.
Sickly… I'm not, though I look like I might be;
I'vegot
the hope of a broken tree trying to be mighty.
Finite as we are we see only slightly, I'm not tumbling
like the weeds though they say the scenery's
nice. And twice, I wished I'd danced to the beat
with which I wrestle rhythm's fight. But tonight…
I'm glad
I'm glad I saved my dance, though my feet are spent,
Exhausted celebration at peril's relent,
Much like the birth of the intangible,
It overwhelms to the point of transcending pain
In hind sight manageable,
The tumultuous and unbearable become mere
turbulent
ecstasy
Sweet Jesus, deliverance!
The beginning of the best of me
The unseen appearance
Intangible testing me
Finding strength in a God,
when nothing was left in me
There was nothing of me
A shell
a supposed to be
You would say a ghost of me
The ugly, hurting, broken me
What am I supposed to be
Emptied out and open me
Then the Lord, He spoke to me
Poured a little Hope in me
The Hoping of a Broken tree

See the things I cannot see
Turn the crap to potpourri
The storm provides no rest for me
Brave the rain, the snow, and sleet
stand my ground
Survive the grind
With God's hand and gift of time
stumped as I am I can still hope to climb.
And If I plunge to earthen floor
I'll never cease to hope for more,
Fire's threat can't wean away
The hope I have to rise one day
Not just hope but hope fulfilled
Nothing strengthens faith like hope distilled
Potent hope will not fail
So the knock of hail from last nights gale
will only serve to prune
Unveil,
The inner me, the inner free
A broken tree? A growing tree!
An understanding, knowing tree
Wisdom from the roots to get what God was showing
me.
When I mooooannnn and when I creek
I'm a Snap back from a bowing tree
And what you think you know you see
And when I moooannnn and I creek
I'm gon' wake you from your potent sleep.
With a mind like cypress knees reaching up to the
glorious light
I stretch forth for the breath of the breeze
And when I moooan you'll hear me speak
And way from inside, I'll bring forth my fruit,
un-retired and Hope inspired

Printed in the United States
by Baker & Taylor Publisher Services